IN T
and

Colin Young

ARTHUR H. STOCKWELL LTD.
Torrs Park   Ilfracombe   Devon
Established 1898
www.ahstockwell.co.uk

© Colin Young, 2004
First published in Great Britain, 2004
All rights reserved.
*No part of this publication may be reproduced
or transmitted in any form or by any means,
electronic or mechanical, including photocopy,
recording, or any information storage and
retrieval system, without permission
in writing from the copyright holder.*

*British Library Cataloguing-in-Publication Data.
A catalogue record for this book is available
from the British Library.*

By the same author:
*It shouldn't happen to a musician
Before it all went wrong*

ISBN 0 7223 3595-4
*Printed in Great Britain by
Arthur H. Stockwell Ltd.
Torrs Park   Ilfracombe
Devon*

Contents

In the Lay-by	5
Bin Laden in My Garden	6
Banana Road	8
The Day I Got Up For Nothing	9
Me and My Dog	10
The Third World	11
My Car	12
A Dreary Day	13
A Wife Compliments Her Husband	14
My Favourite Phrase	15
Thoughts of a General Labourer	16
The Vacuum and Broom	17
The Dream	18
The Writer From Norwich	19
Procrastination	20
The Blade of Grass	21
The Day I Kicked the Wall	22
Breakfast Without a Table	23
Missing the Party	24
The Barber and the Sparrow	25
Drawing The Curtain	26
The Job Dodger	27
The Day I Was Sacked	28
Returning From Tea Break	29
George and Tony	30
The Tired Old Man	32
My Search For a Space	33
The Day Before the Lord's Return	38
Come Back Dark Woods	39
Only Some of Them Do	40
Letters of Rejection	41
Nearly	42

In the Lay-by

My eyes were weary, my arms were aching
And the journey had become quite a test.
I saw a small lay-by not far ahead
And I stopped there for a rest.

It seemed that I were the only one
With nowhere to go in mind,
For dozens of cars went hurtling by,
Leaving me so far behind.

But there were trees to my left and a field or two
Where some sheep were peacefully grazing,
And on that bright day in the middle of May,
I found their beauty to be quite amazing.

I forgot all about the clatter of the traffic
As it all went roaring on by,
And with trees, fields and sheep set beside me,
I daydreamed, carefree as a cloud in the sky.

Bin Laden in My Garden

I got up one morning to water my garden,
Stepped outside and saw Bin Laden.
He was trying to hide behind a tree,
But was all too clear for me to see.

At first, I thought of calling the police,
For I knew him to be a wanted man,
But for ten long days there had been no rain,
And all of the plants were in need of a drink,
Including a sunflower, held up by a cane.

"Good morning, Osama," I said to Bin Laden.
"I'll give you five pounds if you'll water my garden."
Laden agreed and the contract was signed.
I was right to think that he wouldn't mind.

He did a good job, took the money,
Gave me a wink and returned to his van.
"Some say he's bad," I said to my dog,
"But he's still quite good with a watering can!"

One of my neighbours looked over her fence
And saw me in my garden.
"Good morning," she said. "I'm sorry to pry,
But wasn't that Bin Laden I saw in your garden?"

"It certainly was," I said in reply
As I walked up to the fence.
"Why he's in England I really don't know.
It's nice of him to visit my garden though."

"Shouldn't we call the police?" she asked.
"Isn't Bin Laden a wanted man?"
"He certainly is," I said in reply
As I leaned on the fence and took off my tie,
"But the police already have plenty to do.
They wouldn't have time for Osama Bin Laden.
Crime is soaring like never before,
So I gave him five pounds to water my garden."

"I suppose you're probably right," she said
As she looked at my roses and scratched her head.
"With all those speeding vans and cars,
And people breaking the Highway Code,
Dangerous driving, illegal parking,
Children playing football in the middle of the road . . .
Yes indeed, you're probably right.
They wouldn't have time for Osama Bin Laden.
I wouldn't say 'no' to his autograph though,
If he ever comes back to your garden."

Banana Road

I know a road that's full of potholes,
The name of which is 'Banana Road'.
The potholes there are wide and deep,
And the greatest that speeding tyres have sowed.

I took a friend to see them one day.
In amazement she did stand and stare.
Her mouth dropped open and she slowly said,
"Potholes this big are very rare."

Bits of Tarmac flew around
As a car zoomed past, disturbing the road.
A couple of bits hit my girlfriend's face
As a brand-new pothole took its place.

She wiped away the blood on her cheek
And dried her watery eyes.
"I want to go home," she said in pain,
"And don't ever bring me here again!"

"Have you seen the holes in Melon Street?"
I asked as I drove her home,
And when my friend made no reply
I went on to say with a weary sigh,
"They're rather good and I've counted them all.
There are nine or ten of them all in a row."
My friend, however, made it quite clear
That she did not want to know.

The Day I Got Up For Nothing

I got up one morning to build a shed,
But seeing that one had already been built,
I called it a day and went back to bed.

Me and My Dog

I wrote a poem on the first day of spring,
For I had nothing else better to do.
It took three hours and twenty-one minutes,
And then I read it all through.

It made no sense and did not rhyme,
And I said to my dog, "What a waste of time!
It's taken me ages to write this verse
And what I have written is not worth a dime!"

A new idea crept into my mind
As I sat so sadly upon my bed.
With renewed inspiration I picked up my pen
And started to write a novel instead.

Ten years later, I wrote the last page
And put in the last full stop,
But when, at last, I read it all through,
I judged it to be a worthless flop,
And my dog just lay at the foot of the stairs
And did not seem to care.

"I think it is time to hang up my pen,"
I said to my dog that day,
But my dog just barked and picked up his ball,
For he just wanted to play.

The Third World

It must be exciting to travel through space,
To fly the space shuttle all over the place,
To newly discover undiscovered new worlds,
To tread as yet untrodden ground,
To venture into that strange dark world
With no sunlight, no air, no gravity, no sound.

But exciting as it may well be,
Let us not take off too soon.
Until the Third World have enough to eat,
Could we postpone the next trip to the moon?

My Car

If a car could possibly run upon junk,
What a wonderful car mine would be!
There are piles of junk on every seat,
More rubbish than the eye can see.

You would be quite right if you ever did say
That my car resembles a cluttered tip,
But I bet you any money it's the only car in town
That could pass as a mobile skip.

A Dreary Day

It was just another day at work,
And an air of despair was hanging around
Like a big black cloud in the sky overhead,
Beneath which the workers sadly worked,
Drunk with fatigue and nearly half-dead.

It was then that this poem came to my mind
And it proved to be a slight relief.
It saw me through the rest of the day
And slightly reduced my boredom and grief.

It made a change from Elgar's 'Nimrod'
In seeing me through a dismal hour,
And in writing about a dreary day,
That's just about all I can manage to say.

A Wife Compliments Her Husband

A wife arose from her bed one day
To find her husband making some tea.
"I'm gasping for a drink," she said.
"Could you make a cup for me?"

"I'm afraid I can't," he said in reply
As he brought the domestic dog to heel.
"I might be good in bed," he said,
"But I'm hopeless behind a potter's wheel."

"I meant 'a cup of tea'," she said
As she put a star on the Christmas tree,
"And although you're completely hopeless in bed,
You still make a very nice cup of tea."

My Favourite Phrase

Whenever I am lost for words,
Unaware of what I should say,
I always resort to my favourite phrase,
'What a lovely midsummer's day!'

It works quite well in the middle of May
And is perfect for the end of June,
But whenever I say it in the middle of winter,
By five or six months I say it too soon.

Thoughts of a General Labourer

Another day, another bin,
Behind which I find my long-lost broom.
Forget the party. Cancel the ball.
It looks like I won't get the sack after all.

The Vacuum and Broom

Henry, the vacuum, was feeling distraught,
Being used so often for cleaning the floor.
He wanted more time to do his own thing.
He wanted to paint. He wanted to draw.

"I've had enough!" he said at last,
And fled from the house without a sound.
He knew that life was tough out there,
But he was through with being pushed around.

He met a broom, on his way to the coast,
Who had suffered in a similar way,
And together they travelled through country and town.
Perhaps you might see them one day.

The Dream

I was making my way to work one day,
Towards the other side of town,
And what joy I felt, as I left my car,
To find that the place had been burnt down!

But then, an alarm went off beside me,
Somewhere to the left of my nice, warm bed.
It was time to get up and go to work.
"It was all a dream!" I woefully said.

The Writer From Norwich

Oh, that wonderful writer from Norwich,
Who lived to a ripe old age.
He wrote his autobiography
And each day had its very own page.

And when he was young, he was young,
And when he was old, he was old,
And when he had reached his very last day,
His lunch was all mouldy and cold.

Procrastination

I noticed how long my nails were,
As I sat on the toilet one day,
And I thought that I ought to trim them a bit,
But felt more tired than words can say,
So in the end I went back to bed
And left the task for another day.

The Blade of Grass

"I enjoy my life as a blade of grass,"
Said one blade of grass to another.
"I enjoy the sun and the light summer breeze,
And it's nice to hear the birds in the trees,
But along with all the joys of my life
A fear still haunts me in my warm sunny glade.
Far worse than being trodden on
Is to be cut down by a lawn mower's blade!"

The Day I Kicked the Wall

I was feeling a bit annoyed one day,
But did not wish to be cruel,
So I turned a blind eye to the cat and the dog,
And instead I kicked the wall.

Breakfast Without a Table

There we both were, having breakfast,
A few fried eggs and a bit of bread.
My friend returned her plate to the floor.
"The floor is far too low," she said.

We had both the chairs, but lacked the table,
So breakfast, that morning, was a troublesome thing.
My friend bent down to pick up her cup.
"The floor is far too low," she said,
"And I'm sorry, to have to say it again,
But the floor's too low to serve as a table,
And is putting my back under terrible strain!"

"You might be right," I said in reply
As I returned my cup to the floor.
"I'm sure that I am," she said on leaving,
And as she left, she slammed the door.

"Women!" I said to Spot, my dog.
"Why do they always complain?"
I bought a table later that day,
But by the time I got back home,
She had left on the six o'clock train.

Missing the Party

I wanted some peace, but instead got noise,
Noise from the party in the room down below.
"Come on down," my friend had said,
But I wanted some peace and so I said, "No."

"You will miss all the sex," my friend had said.
"Do come down to the party below."
I wanted, however, to read a book,
And I wanted some peace and so I said, "No."

The Barber and the Sparrow

The barber was feeling rather frustrated,
So he went outside and kicked a few trees.
He returned to the chair and said to the sparrow,
"Will you keep your head still, please?"

The sparrow, however, did not understand
And kept on moving its head.
The barber finally threw down his scissors.
"I wish I had stayed in bed," he said.

Drawing the Curtain

I couldn't be bothered to draw the curtain,
So instead, I drew the curtain
And stuck the drawing right onto the pane,
Which delayed the task for certain.

My depression was deep, the very next day
When it dawned on me, at half-past eight,
That it would have been easier just to draw the curtain
And now, of course, it was all too late.

The Job Dodger

He prayed for the flu to hit him hard,
For he didn't know what else to do.
He certainly didn't want the job
And preferred to have the flu.

The agency rang him, the very next day.
"Where on earth are you?" they cried out loud.
"I'm in bed with the flu," he said in reply,
"And you can give the job to another guy."

The Day I Was Sacked

I pulled the chain to flush the toilet
And leaned against the wall.
I made no haste to wash my hands.
I did not rush at all.

I like to listen to the sounds of the cistern
Just after I've pulled the chain,
And it's nice to have a moment's rest
Before trudging back to my job once again.

I walked to the sink, washed my hands
And started my slow return,
But as I went back, the foreman said,
"Clock out you clown, for you've got the sack!"

The reason for dismissal was unknown to myself,
And I had no wish to know.
I used my clock card for the final time,
And it felt so nice to be able to go.

The rain had been falling for many hours
And every field resembled a bog,
But I kept to the paths as I went back home,
Relieved, delighted, full of joy
And as happy as a flea on a dog.

Returning From Tea Break

The tea break was over, and we all knew it well,
As we rose from our chairs at the sound of the bell.

We left the canteen with grumpy faces
And started to trudge back to work.
"We need an earthquake," said George to Fred.
"I need to go back to bed," I said.

I was walking behind the oldest worker
Who was slowing me down so well.
At times like these, the older workers
Are worth more than words can tell.

"Do get a move on," the manager shouted,
"For we really don't have all day!
The job must be finished by the end of April,
And not by the end of May!"

The oldest worker went no faster.
He had reached his limit already,
And lacking the strength to overtake,
I maintained the speed of a dying drake.

The manager grimaced, shook his head,
Tutted and looked at his watch.
"I've had enough of this!" he said,
And went outside, not only to smoke,
But also to drink his Scotch.

George and Tony

"I do hope my dog comes back," said George,
"And I don't know why she left,
But most of her fleas are now on me
And of my blood they are guilty of theft.
So many baths do I take each day,
And the bills for my laundry soar sky-high.
If my dog does not return quite soon,
Then a new one I shall have to buy."

"You might as well have mine," said Tony.
"I am bored with walking him anyway.
My dog won't mind as long as he's fed,
And taken for a walk four times a day."

Quite overcome with sudden joy,
George gave Tony a wild kiss.
"Be careful," said Tony. "Not in the park,
And don't forget that I'm male.
People will talk and rumours will spread
Through village and town, valley and dale."

"I'm sorry," said George, slightly embarrassed,
"I forgot we were in the park."
"Well don't," said Tony, "or people will talk
And dogs will start to bark!"

"I forgot you were male as well," said George.
"Thanks for your kind and generous offer."
"You're more than welcome," Tony replied.
"I am bored with walking him, as I say.
Pedigree Chum is his favourite dish,
And keep him away from your garden pond,
For he's also fond of fish."

Thus it was that Tony's dog
Went to live with George that day,
And on the subject of Tony and George,
That's just about all that I have to say.

The Tired Old Man

A tired old man got up one morning
To write his final poem,
But seeing that the job had already been done,
And recalling that he wrote it the night before,
He called it a day, went back to bed,
Died at noon and wrote no more.

My Search For a Space

"I'm looking for a space," I said
To a man in charge of a merry-go-round.
"I have looked for a space all over the place,
But no space have I found."

"There ain't no spaces here," he said,
"For you're right in the midst of a big, busy fair."
"I suppose you're right," I said with a sigh,
And wandered away in the depths of despair.

I asked a parrot if he could help,
As he ate some seed from out of his tray,
But he stared at me as though I were mad,
And clearly had nothing to say.

I left the parrot with a weary sigh,
And continued my search for a space,
But wherever I looked, the ground was packed
With objects and people all over the place.

I asked a clown if he could help,
As he sat, on his own, behind a few stalls.
"I can't quite think at the moment," he said,
"For I'm busy juggling my balls."

"You just juggle your balls," I said,
And continued my search for a space,
But nothing had changed for it was all the same,
With objects and people all over the place.

I asked a policeman, but he was no help,
And the tramps just drank their whisky.
I wanted to ask the candyfloss man,
But the queue for him was the length of Iran.

I came across a fortune-teller
As she sat behind her crystal ball.
"Hello," I said. "I am seeking a space.
Do you know of any suitable place?"

She put down her coffee, closed her book
And gave me a friendly smile.
"You look worn out," she said with a sigh.
"I'm nearly half-dead," I said in reply.

"It's a very big world," she went on to say,
"And I'm sure there must be a space somewhere,
But it won't be easy to find one here
For you're right in the midst of a big, busy fair."

"You've got to help me," I said in despair,
"For the crowds are driving me mad.
I can scarcely afford my therapy bills,
And my whole situation is terribly sad."

"Take a seat," she said in reply,
"And don't get into a flap.
Sit on the chair and try to relax,
Or I'll have to give you a slap."

The threat of the slap calmed me down
As I took my place in the chair,
And I started to wish that I had not come
To this crowded and dreadful fair.

She opened a drawer, took out a duster
And dusted her crystal ball.
"It has to be free of dust," she said,
"Or it will be no help at all."

She gazed into her crystal ball
And waited for the mist to clear.
"I see a space," she said at last,
"And I think it's not too far from here."

"But where?" I cried. "Where is this space?
Please let me know just as soon as you can.
I have looked for a space for hours on end,
And I've come to be a desperate man!"

A little annoyed, she rose from her chair
And gave me a slap to calm me down.
She sipped some water, wiped her hands
And sat back down with a bit of a frown.

"I need some time," she said with a sigh,
And then she closed her eyes.
She slowly caressed her crystal ball
And then she said after two more sighs,

"The multistorey car park. The space lies there,
And it's only two or three miles ahead."
I took my pipe from out of my mouth.
"Now that makes a change for sure," I said.

"It certainly does," she said in reply,
"But I tell you sincerely that I'm far from wrong.
Make haste. Go quickly. Waste no time,
For spaces in car parks don't last long."

Deeply grateful, I gave her a hug
And also a wild and wanton kiss.
"Go," she said, "before it's too late.
Spaces like these are too good to miss."

"How much do I owe you?" I joyfully asked
As I took out my wallet and opened it up.
"Put it away," she said in reply.
"You have paid me with a kiss,
And go straight away at a tiger's pace.
It would be quite sad if you missed this space."

I embraced her wildly one more time
And on this occasion we fell to the floor.
Her husband came in, pulled me off her,
Gave me a slap and showed me the door.

He kicked me out with a size twelve foot,
And I landed on top of a wall.
My thoughts, however, were fixed on the space,
So I did not mind at all.

I jumped off the wall and ran to the car park
In order to look for the vital space,
And a tiger on steroids could not have ran faster
As I knocked people down all over the place.

I arrived at the car park as the sun was setting,
And I found the space on the very top floor,
But my heart was filled with utter despair
When I saw and read a notice there.

'Disabled persons only' it said,
And amazed at my hardship, I scratched my head.
I gave up my search and returned to my house,
And I hoped that there might be a space in my bed.

The Day Before the Lord's Return

I caught the bus to work that day
And arrived at half-past eight.
Most of the staff were there on time
And the same old few were late.

I took my breaks at their normal time
And went back home at half-past four.
My dog was glad to see my return,
And wagged his tail when I opened the door.

I ate my tea and played the piano,
Desirous of J. S. Bach,
And after reading a bit of my book
I walked my dog around the park.

I then made plans for the following day
From the start to finish, all the way through,
And of what was about to take place in the world,
Like everyone else, I hadn't a clue.

Come Back Dark Woods

I wandered through a city centre
As darkness was falling to start the night.
I saw the empty bottles and cans,
The broken glass and a vicious fight.

I saw the loud and zooming skateboards
And heard the swearing all around.
I saw the graffiti on every wall
And the vomit on the ground.

I saw the pretty damsels
With their skirts as short as my comb.
I tried my best to look elsewhere
And wished I had stayed at home.

I entered a pub to buy a pint
Where a noisy quarrel was in full swing.
Someone hit me and I fell to the floor.
Come back dark woods, for you scare me no more.

Only Some of Them Do

If you're due to be joined in marriage
And sick with worry, you lack the strength
To get out of bed, to brush your teeth,
To comb your hair or mount your horse,
Then be consoled and don't despair
For not all marriages end in divorce.

Letters of Rejection

If only a job were as easy to get
As a letter of the strictest rejection,
I could stop filling in all the tiring forms
And go for a walk instead,
But I have no need to buy any paper
To cover my large and naked walls,
For I'll use my letters of rejection instead,
And shall look at them fondly every night
Before I return to my Slumberland bed,
And trust that my future will be all right
In my Maker's capable hands.

Nearly

I was nearly dismissed from work one day
For losing my dustpan and brush,
And as I laboured through the rest of the day
I said to my friends, Veronica Bush,
Sarah Brown and Margaret Clay,
"Forget the champagne. Cancel the ball.
Forget the party on Saturday night,
For although I was nearly sacked today,
'Nearly' still means 'not quite'."

Veronica Bush bought me a coffee
And Sarah gave me a biscuit.
"Never you mind," said Margaret Clay,
"For it might still happen another day."